A
Laurel Burch
CHRISTMAS

BLISS and BLESSINGS

MANY MOMENTS of MAGIC MAKING

a TREASURE · TROVE · of · TREATS

C&T PUBLISHING

Text and artwork© 2004 C&T Publishing

Artwork © 2004 Laurel Burch

Editors: Cyndy Lyle Rymer, Lynn Koolish

Technical Editor: Catherine Comyns, Katrina Lamken, Gael Betts

Copyeditor/Proofreader: Katrina Lamken, Sarah Sacks Dunn,
    Susan Nelsen

Cover Designer: Kristy A. Konitzer

Design Director/Book Designer: Kristy A. Konitzer

Illustrators: Mary Ann Tenorio, Nancy Lorenz

Production Assistant: Kirstie L. McCormick

Photography: All photography by Diane Pedersen,
    Kirstie L. McCormick, and Luke Mulks unless otherwise noted

Published by C&T Publishing, Inc., P.O. Box 1456, Lafayette,
    California 94549

Cover photo: Santa Paws Pillow made by Barbara Baker and Jeri Boe,
    Bend Oregon

Back cover: Surprise-a-Day Tree Calendar made by Catherine Comyns,
    Pleasant Hill, Ca

Many thanks to the Richardson family for allowing us to create Christmas in their home in July, and to Megan and Mickey for being such great models. Thanks also to Franki and Mendelssohn Kohler.

Attention Copy Shops: Please note the following exception—Publisher and author give permission to photocopy pages 10-12, 18-19, 31, 34-35, 37-39, 42, 44, 47, 50, 52, 53, 55, 56, 62, 67, and 70 for personal use only.

Attention Teachers: C&T Publishing, Inc. encourages you to use this book as a text for teaching. Contact us at 800-284-1114 or www.ctpub.com for more information about the C&T Teachers Program.

We take great care to ensure that the information included in this book is accurate and presented in good faith, but no warranty is provided nor results guaranteed. Having no control over the choices of materials or procedures used, neither the author nor C&T Publishing, Inc., shall have any liability to any person or entity with respect to any loss or damage caused directly or indirectly by the information contained in this book. For your convenience, we post an up-to-date listing of corrections on our Web page (www.ctpub.com). If a correction is not already noted, please contact our customer service department at ctinfo@ctpub.com or at P.O. Box 1456, Lafayette, California 94549.

Trademarked (™) and Registered Trademark (®) names are used throughout this book. Rather than use the symbols with every occurrence of a trademark and registered trademark name, we are using the names only in the editorial fashion and to the benefit of the owner, with no intention of infringement.

Library of Congress Cataloging-in-Publication Data

Burch, Laurel.
  A Laurel Burch Christmas : color the season beautiful with 25 quilts & crafts / Laurel Burch.
     p. cm.
  Includes bibliographical references and index.
  ISBN 1-57120-247-1 (paper trade)
  1. Patchwork--Patterns. 2. Machine appliqué--Patterns. 3. Machine quilting. 4. Christmas decorations. I. Title.

TT835.B817 2004
  746.46'041--dc22
2004000338

Printed in China

10 9 8 7 6 5 4 3 2

To my beautiful girls,
Aarin, Melonie, and Karly,
who love every little ribbon,
bow and embellishment I fuss
over painstakingly when
conjuring up my creative magic...
Being appreciated is the ultimate inspiration!

And to Rick Sara, my life partner, who brings
so much joy and comfort to each and every day,
and to C&T, the quintessential publishers who
bring ideas and magic to reality, for all to share
and enjoy.

Blessings

Laurel Burch

Contents

Gorgeous Gifts...7

Surprise-a-Day...15

Peace Moon...21

Village of Blessings...25

Matisse & Tiger...29

Giving Joy...33

Stocking Full of Merry Critters...36

Magical Winged Bunny...41

Bearly Christmas...43

Santa Paws...45

Dancing Dogs Mantel Runner...49

Joyful Cats Tree Skirt...51

Very Special Ornament Collection...54

Starlight Forest Table Runner and Placemats...59

Dear Santa Tote Bag...65

Wings of a Dove Felt Wreath...68

Tips & Techniques for Appliqué and Embellishments...72

Resources...78

Index...78

About the Author...80

A Season of Blessings

Counting blessings and expressing gratitude
can happen in many ways.

When i paint, it is my way of doing this ...
Inspired to express deep appreciation for
the beauty —, abundance, and sacredness
of life —, my art brings this desire —
to it's fullest fruition —.

Some paintings, like this one —
are like little offerings to the world
in a kind of global language —~
the bird symbolizing peace and harmony.
loving arms holding all living beings
in a safe place —.
When i finish these little offerings
i close my eyes and send them off to you ..
that they may touch your heart —
in a way that you, too, will want to
pass them on in the world as a gesture of
appreciation and gratitude for someone else.
May love and peace be with you —.

Laurel ♥

Finished Quilt Size: 53" x 77"

Machine appliquéd and quilted by Christine Taylor, Pleasanton, CA, 2003. Fabric generously donated by Marcus Brothers.

Photo by Sharon Risedorph

Gorgeous Gifts

Materials

- Gray print: 2 yards for filler strips between gift blocks
- Various brights for gift blocks:
  - Blue: ½ yard
  - Purple: ½ yard
  - Red: 1 yard
  - Gold: ¾ yard
  - Teal: 1 yard
  - Black: ⅝ yard
  - Black print: ½ yard
  - Orange: ¾ yard
  - Fuchsia: 1 yard
  - Green: ¼ yard
  - Bronze: ⅛ yard
  - White: ¼ yard for dove and cat's eyes
- Backing: 3⅛ yards
- Binding: Scraps to total ½ yard
- Batting: 57" x 81"
- Fusible web: 3 yards
- Thread: Black and metallic gold, red, and pink
- Metallic gold trim: 8 yards
- Black trim: 3⅜ yards
- Buttons, ½" to ¾" in diameter: 21 red for holly berries, 1 black for dove's eye
- Fabric paint: Black, red, teal, and metallic gold

Cutting

See Tips & Techniques for Appliqué and Embellishments on page 72 for helpful information before you start this or any project.

Gray Print: Cut the filler strips to border each gift block according to the dimensions in the Cutting and Assembly Diagram on page 9.

Various Brights: Cut fabrics for the base of each gift block according to the dimensions in the Cutting and Assembly Diagram. These are the cut sizes and include the seam allowance. We recommend that you cut the block backgrounds larger than the sizes given, then trim to the size shown after the appliqué, paint, and embellishment is complete.

Scraps: Bias-cut random lengths of scraps 1¾" wide to equal 270" for the binding. Cut the ends at a 45° angle.

Fabric for appliqué: Cut as needed.

Tips for Making Gorgeous Gifts

The quilt is assembled in 5 sections.

1. If desired have the patterns on pages 10-12 enlarged 500% before you begin, or use the patterns as guidelines only for placement of design elements. See instructions for machine appliqué using fusible web on pages 72-73. Trace all pattern pieces onto the fusible web. Fuse the web to the wrong side of the appliqué fabric. Cut out the appliqué shapes.

2. Cover your workspace to protect it before painting details on the gift packages. Paint before you start fusing appliqué shapes to the back ground. Let the paint dry completely.

3. For each gift block: Machine piece the shapes (optional) or paint the design onto the gift block fabric.

4. Add the painted geometric shapes and designs, details, and embellishments.

5. Use fusible web appliqués to add decorative shapes such as bows and animals.

6. Use decorative thread to machine appliqué using a simple zigzag or a decorative stitch around each shape. Add decorative trim to cover the pieced seams.

7. Sew the gray print background filler strips to each pieced gift block. Trim each block to the size indicated in the piecing diagram. Arrange the blocks and sew to make each section.

8. Sew the 5 sections together to make the quilt top.

9. Use fusible web to add the decorative details that overlap blocks. Use decorative thread to machine appliqué the remaining decorative details to the quilt top.

10. Layer the quilt top, batting, and backing. Pin or thread-baste the layers together.

11. Quilt as desired. Trim to the finished size. Sew binding strips together with a diagonal seam and bind the quilt.

12. Stitch buttons to the quilt to represent holly berries and the dove's eye.

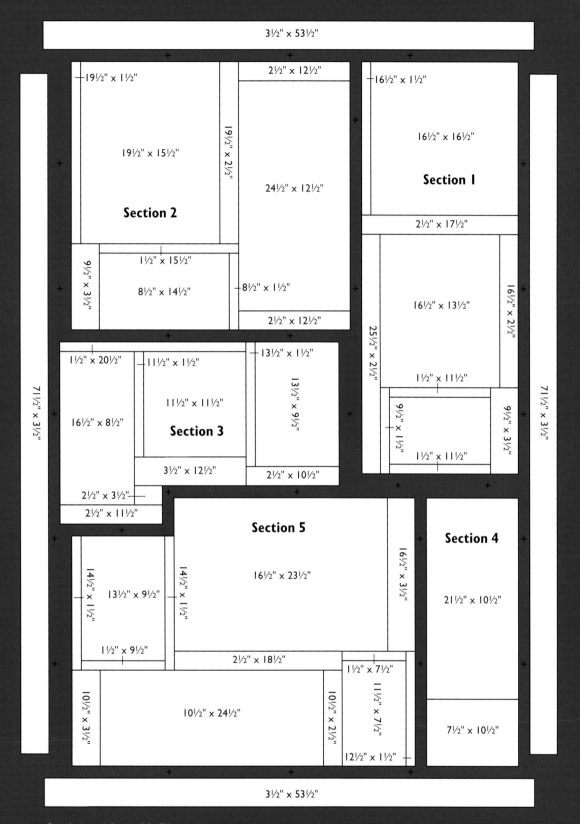

Cutting and Assembly Diagram

Gorgeous Gifts

section 1

section 4

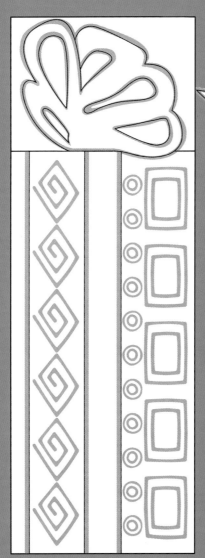

Enlarge 500%.

top

Enlarge 500%.

section 3

section 2

Enlarge 500%.

Surprise-a-Day
Tree Calendar

Finished Quilt Size: 43" x 41"

Machine appliquéd, quilted, and embellished by Catherine Comyns, Pleasant Hill, California, 2003.
"Shimmer" fabrics generously donated by Marcus Brothers.

Materials

- Green: 1¼ yards for background (2½ yards to piece background if fabric is not at least 42" wide)
- Green plaid: 2½ yards for back of ornaments, quilt backing, and binding
- Cotton lamé: 1 yard total of assorted colors for gift pockets and ties

- Black: 1 yard for background of ornaments
- Assorted bright prints and solids to total 1 yard for ornaments
- Batting: 47" x 45"
- Fusible web: 2 yards
- Pinking shears or pinking blade
- Variegated metallic thread for decorative stitching

- Metallic gold ribbon, ¼" wide: 2 yards for attaching ornaments
- Metallic gold ribbon, ½" to ¾" wide: 9 yards for bows on top of gift pockets
- Gold star sequins
- Assorted metallic beads
- Gold fabric pen or fabric paint

Cutting

See Tips & Techniques for Appliqué and Embellishments on page 72 for helpful information before you start this or any project.

Green: Cut (and piece if needed) 1 rectangle 44" wide x 42" high for the tree.

Cotton Lamé: Cut 25 pockets from various cotton lamé fabrics according to the dimensions in the Cutting and Assembly Diagram on page 17.

Cut 10 strips ¾" wide from the lamé fabrics for the gift ties.

Green Plaid: Cut and piece 4 strips 2½" wide for a total of 150" for binding.

Fabric for appliqué: Cut as needed.

Tips for Making Surprise-a-Day Tree

1. Have the patterns on pages 18-19 enlarged 150% before you begin. See instructions for machine appliqué using fusible web on pages 72-73. Trace all pattern pieces onto the fusible web. Fuse the web to the wrong side of the appliqué fabric. Cut out the appliqué shapes.

2. Fold a piece of paper 44" wide by 42" high in half lengthwise. Draw a dot at the top on the

fold, draw a second dot at the lower edge 22" from the center fold. Draw a line between the dots to form half of the triangle tree shape. Cut along the drawn line to create the tree pattern.

Draw the tree outline onto the green batik fabric but do not cut yet.

3. For each of the 25 pockets turn the side edges and bottom edge ¼" to the back and lightly press. Turn the top edge ⅜" to the back. Turn under ⅜" again and sew close to the folded edge.

4. For the gift ties press the long edges to meet in the center of the back of each ¾" wide strip of lamé. Pin the pressed strips to the front of each pocket and trim to the width and length of the pocket. Sew in place close to the pressed edges. Stitch a star sequin and bead to each tie intersection.

5. Pin each pocket to the quilt top referring to the diagram on page 17. Use decorative thread to attach the pocket to the green batik tree. Sew down one side of the pocket, across the bottom, and up the other side, leaving the hemmed top edge open.

6. Layer the quilt top to the batting and backing. Pin or thread-baste the layers together.

7. Outline-quilt around each pocket, being careful not to stitch the pocket closed.

8. Trim the tree to the drawn tree shape and bind.

9. Fuse the black fabric to 1 yard of the green plaid ornament backing fabric. Draw the outline of the ornament shapes onto the fusible web on the back of the assorted bright prints and solids. Cut the shapes and fuse them to the black fabric. Use decorative thread to machine appliqué around each shape. Use pinking shears or a pinking blade to cut the black background ¼" outside each ornament. Use a gold fabric pen or fabric paint to embellish the background ornaments, and the black pinked edging. Stitch beads and sequins to accentuate eyes and other features. Make 25 ornaments of various sizes to fit into the 25 gift pockets.

10. Pin each ornament to the outside of its corresponding pocket. Cut a piece of narrow gold ribbon about 2" long to reach from approximately ½" below the top of the ornament to ½" above the top of its corresponding pocket. For the 3 hearts, circles, or butterflies, extend the ribbon and attach all 3 shapes to it. Fold ¼" under and hand stitch one short end of the ribbon to the back of the ornament. Place the ornament in its pocket. Cut the wide gold ribbon into 12" lengths. Tie each length into a bow. Stitch the bow ⅜" above the top of each pocket, catching the folded ¼" edge of the ribbon extending from the top of the ornament. Embellish the tree with sequins and beads.

Photo by Garry Gay

Surprise-a-Day Tree Calendar

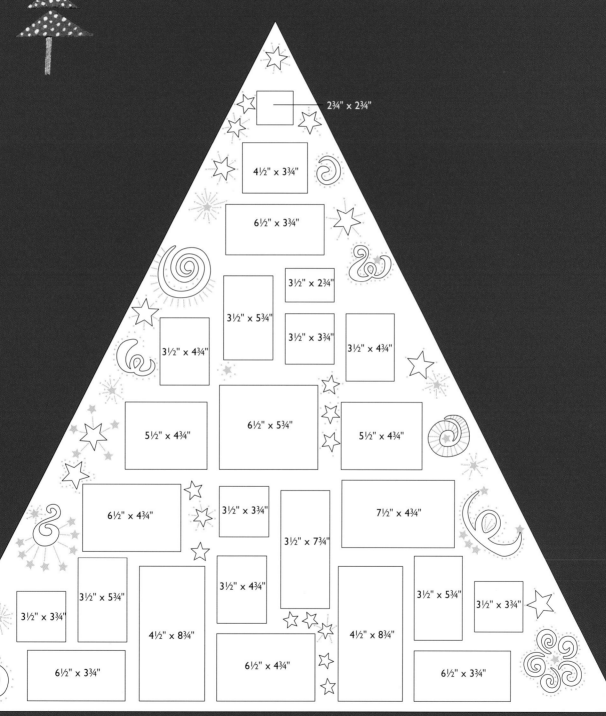

42"

2¾" x 2¾"

4½" x 3¾"

6½" x 3¾"

3½" x 2¾"

3½" x 5¾"

3½" x 4¾"

3½" x 3¾"

3½" x 4¾"

5½" x 4¾"

6½" x 5¾"

5½" x 4¾"

6½" x 4¾"

3½" x 3¾"

7½" x 4¾"

3½" x 7¾"

3½" x 4¾"

3½" x 5¾"

3½" x 3¾"

3½" x 3¾"

3½" x 5¾"

4½" x 8¾"

4½" x 8¾"

6½" x 3¾"

6½" x 4¾"

6½" x 3¾"

44"

Enlarge 150%.

Enlarge 150%.

Peace Moon

Finished Quilt Size: 18" x 26"

Machine appliquéd, quilted, and embellished by Cyndy Lyle Rymer, Danville, CA, 2003. "Shimmer" fabrics generously donated by Marcus Brothers. Silver braid donated by Kreinik Mfg. Inc.

Materials

- Navy blue: 1½ yards for background, backing, and binding
- Silver: 1 fat quarter for moon and stars
- Fuchsia or gradated fabric: ⅛ yard for borders
- Scraps: yellow, fuchsia, several greens, purple, orange, blue, blue-green, turquoise, and white for letters and border pieces
- Batting: 22" x 30"
- Fusible web: 1 yard
- Threads for decorative stitching: Silver metallic, yellow, fuchsia, and turquoise
- Silver paint
- Optional: 4 yards ⅛"-wide silver braid for outlining letters
- Black fabric marker
- Fabric paints: fuchsia, yellow, orange, and silver

Cutting

See Tips & Techniques for Appliqué and Embellishments on page 72 for helpful information before you start this or any project.

Navy blue: Cut 1 rectangle 14½" x 23½" for the base of the quilt.
Cut and piece 3 strips 2½" wide to equal 110" for the binding.

Fuchsia: Cut 1 strip 2" x 23½" for the left side border.
Cut 1 strip 2½" x 25½" for the right side border.
Cut 1 strip 1½" x 16" for the inner bottom border.

Orange: Cut 1 strip 1½" x 11½" for the top border.

Turquoise: Cut 1 strip 1½" x 6½" for the top border.

Blue-green: Cut 1 strip 1½" x 18" for the outer bottom border.

Fabric for appliqué: Cut as needed.

Tips for Making Peace Moon

1. A full size pattern is on the pullout at the back of the book. See instructions for machine appliqué using fusible web on page 72. Trace all pattern pieces onto the fusible web following the instructions on page 73.

2. Cover your workspace to protect it before painting. Using the heavy gray lines on the pattern as guidelines paint before you start fusing appliqué shapes to the background. Let the paint dry completely. **Note:** Add the painted silver dots <u>after</u> the quilt top is assembled.

3. Lightly draw in all of the details on the appliqué pieces, such as the eye on the moon and the feathers on the birds' wings.

4. Use blue-green base fabric for the bird on the left-bottom corner. Sponge-paint with yellow, orange, and purple. After the paint dries, fuse on a white beak and draw details with the black fabric marker. Use blue fabric for the wing of the bird on the bottom right, and paint with yellow-green and yellow.

5. Layer the flower pieces and then fuse together.

6. Fuse the green tendrils and holly leaves onto the lower right side of the moon. Leave the paper backing on the portions of the tendril and leaf that will extend into the border. Fuse these after the border strips are added. Fuse the lips. Using a stem stitch, embroider the eyelashes onto the moon using heavy silver thread, or by couching silver trim. Stem-stitch a black curved line above the eye to give it definition. Fuse the flowers in place on the moon.

7. Assemble the quilt top. Sew the left side border to the navy base.

   Piece the orange and turquoise strips using a diagonal seam. Trim to fit your quilt and sew to the top of the quilt.

   Add the inner bottom border, the right side border, and the outer bottom border.

8. Fuse the moon in place. Fuse the remainder of the tendril and holly leaf.

9. Fuse the birds onto the base. Use a stem stitch or narrow satin stitch to create the birds' legs and feet.

10. Fuse the letters and stars in place. Outline the letters with silver metallic thread and satin stitching around each letter, or use fusible metallic braid to outline the letters.

11. Layer the quilt top, batting and backing. Pin or thread-baste the layers together.

12. Quilt around the moon, stars, leaves, tendrils, letters, birds, and flowers. Quilt in the border following the design shown in the quilt photo.

13. Trim to the finished size and bind.

14. Add small dots with silver paint around the moon, stars, and letters.

Treasures Trunk

Materials

- Any size wooden or papier-maché box
- Small wooden stars, available at most craft stores
- Navy spray paint
- Silver spray paint
- Painter's tape (usually blue)
- Small foam brush
- Silver acrylic paint
- Tacky white glue or hot glue gun
- New pencil

Here's a fun, easy project to make to store a young child's treasures, or your own. All it takes are an unfinished wooden box, some spray paint, and unpainted wooden stars.

Tips for Making a Treasures Trunk

1. Remove or cover any hardware with painter's tape.

2. Spray the entire box with the navy blue paint. Let dry.

3. Spray the stars with the silver paint. Let dry.

4. Hold the silver spray can about 2' away from the wooden box, and gently spray. You don't want to cover the navy blue paint, just add small silver spots. Let dry.

5. Use a new pencil eraser and the silver acrylic paint to make dots along all sides of the corners of the box. Paint spirals on the box.

6. Glue stars onto wooden box.

7. Re-attach the hardware.

8. Fill with your most precious treasures.

Finished Quilt Size: 28" x 20"

Machine appliquéd, pieced, quilted, and embellished by Nancy Odom, Westfield, Indiana, 2003.
Fabric generously donated by Benartex Inc. Radiance "Frize" yarn generously donated by Quilters' Resource, Inc.
Photo by Garry Gay

Village of Blessings

Materials

- Black batik: ½ yard for background
- A variety of bright prints and solids to total 1 yard
- Backing: ¾ yard
- Binding: ¼ yard
- Batting: 32" x 24"
- Fusible web: 2 yards
- Radiance "Frize" yarn (see Resources): 10 yards of ⅛"-wide gold, green, black, or metallic gold trim
- Metallic black trim: 15 yards of ⅛"-wide
- Gold bugle beads, 4.5 mm: 20
- Assorted colored beads in a variety of sizes: 150
- Optional: Gold beads, 2 mm: 200
- Gold metallic pen, fine-point

Cutting

See Tips & Techniques for Appliqué and Embellishments on page 72 for helpful information before you start this or any project.

Black: Cut 1 rectangle 24¼" x 16¼" for the background.

Assorted Prints and Solids: Cut 2 strips 1" x 16¼" for the inner side borders.
Cut 2 strips 2½" x 16¼" for the outer side borders.

Cut 2 strips ⅞" x 29" for the inner top and bottom borders.
Cut 2 strips 2½" x 24½" for the outer top and bottom borders.
Cut 2 strips 1" x 2½" for the outer top and bottom sashing.
Cut 4 squares 2½" x 2½" for the corner posts.
Cut as needed for appliqué shapes

Binding: Cut and piece 3 strips 2¼" wide for a total of 106".

Tips for Making Village of Blessings

1. A full-size pattern is on the pullout at the back of the book. See instructions for machine appliqué using fusible web on pages 72-73. Trace all pattern pieces onto the fusible web.

2. Cover your workspace to protect it before painting. Paint before you start fusing appliqué shapes to the background. Let the paint dry completely.

3. After fusing the web to the wrong side of the fabric cut out the shapes. Fuse and machine appliqué the shapes onto the background.

4. Use metallic threads to sew details onto the animal shapes and buildings. Sew metallic trim around each shape. Add beads to embellish the shapes.

5. Using the heavy gray lines on the pattern as guidelines use the gold metallic pen to add details to the borders, building, animals, and foreground.

6. Layer the quilt top with the batting and backing. Pin or thread-baste the layers together.

7. Quilt as desired. Trim to the finished size and bind.

8. Optional: Hand-stitch gold beads to further embellish the quilt.

Kindred Spirits
... Another soul
    resonating with yours

— A dance of life between beings.

At Christmas time
all my animals are lovingly tied
with ribbons and bows, bells and
bright red holly berries and leaves.

Their steps are more lively!
They know it is a special time
    and companions like my beloved
dog Matisse know they are part of it!

Let all hearts be merry and bright!

♡ love, Laurel

♡ this image was inspired by
my cat, Tiger and
my black lab, Matisse ...
who both bring such great
joy to me, every day   !

Matisse & Tiger

Finished Quilt Size: 24" x 30"

Machine appliquéd, quilted and embellished by Gailen Runge, Oakland, California, 2003.
Fabric generously donated by Marcus Brothers.

Materials

- White cotton lamé: 2 yards for background, backing, and binding
- Gray cotton lamé: 3/8 yard for dog
- Silver cotton lamé: 3/8 yard for cat
- Red cotton lamé: 1/4 yard for ribbon
- Green cotton lamé: 1/4 yard for ribbon
- Batting: 28" x 34"
- Fusible web: 1 1/2 yards
- Metallic gold ribbon: 3 1/4 yards of 1/2"-wide for frame
- Thread for decorative stitching: Gold and black
- Metallic gold trim: 8 yards of 1/8"-wide
- Black bias tape: 8 yards of 1/4"-wide
- Fabric paint: Silver, white, black, orange, yellow, dark green, light green, purple, gold, pink, and turquoise

Cutting

See Tips & Techniques for Appliqué and Embellishments on page 72 for helpful information before you start this or any project.

White Cotton Lamé: Cut 2 rectangles 28" x 34" for the background and backing.

Binding: Cut and piece 3 strips 2 1/4" wide for a total of 120".

Tips for Making Matisse & Tiger

1. Have the pattern on page 31 enlarged 277% before you begin. See instructions for machine appliqué using fusible web on page 73. Trace all pattern pieces onto the fusible web.

2. Cover your workspace to protect it before painting. Using the heavy gray lines on the pattern as guidelines, paint before you start fusing appliqué shapes to the background. Let the paint dry completely.

3. Sew gold ribbon onto the quilt top to create a 19 1/2" x 27" frame.

4. Carefully fuse the animal shapes to the quilt top.

5. Use decorative thread to machine appliqué and embellish the shapes.

6. Outline the bandanas and animals with the black bias tape.

7. Outline the facial details with the narrow gold braid.

8. Add additional painted embellishments.

9. Layer the quilt top with the batting and backing. Pin or thread-baste the layers together.

10. Quilt around the shapes and ribbon frame. Quilt floral shapes in the body of the cat.

11. Quilt the details as desired. Trim to finished size and bind.

A Bandana for a Best Friend

While you are decking the halls this holiday season, why not make one of these bandanas for your dog or cat? All it takes is a square of fabric, some star stencils you can make with freezer paper, and acrylic paint.

Materials

- Square of fabric about 18" x 18" for a cat or small dog, or about 25" x 25" or larger for bigger animals
- Fabric paint (silver was used to make this bandana)
- Freezer paper
- Craft knife
- Small foam brush
- Chunky pencil with eraser
- Swirl rubber stamp

Mendelssohn, who lives with Franki and David Kohler, looks very debonair in his custom-made Laurel Burch bandana.

Tips for Making the Bandana

1. Fold the edges of the square under ¼", and fold again. Stitch fold in place. Press. Fold the bandana in half diagonally and press.

2. Trace the stars on page 53 or any other patterns on the paper side of freezer paper.

3. Use the craft knife to cut out several stars or other shapes from the freezer paper to create stencils. Leave 1" or more on all sides of the stencil.

4. Iron the shiny side of the freezer paper stencil to the folded bandana. Use just a little of the acrylic paint—your brush should be almost dry—to paint the stencils. Let dry.

5. Lift the freezer paper and move to another area of the bandana and repeat step 4.

6. Dip the eraser end of the pencil into the acrylic paint and paint dots along the outside edge of the bandana. Let dry.

MATISSE & TIGER   31

Giving Joy

Finished Quilt Size: 48" x 24"

Machine appliquéd, quilted, and embellished by Nancy Busby,
Rio Vista, CA, 2003. Fabrics generously donated by Benartex Inc.

Materials

- Black: 1½ yards for background
- Various bright scraps: to total ½ yard for trees and gifts
- Backing: 1½ yards
- Binding: ⅓ yard
- Batting: 52" x 28"

- Fusible web: 1½ yards
- Thread for decorative stitching: Gold metallic
- Metallic braid: 8 yards of ⅛"-wide assorted colors
- Metallic puff paint: Gold, silver, blue, red, yellow, pink, and purple

- Crystal gems in assorted sizes and colors: 60
- Sequins, 9 mm, in assorted colors: 20
- Beads, 2 mm, in assorted colors: 250
- Fabric glue or hot glue gun

Cutting

See Tips & Techniques for Appliqué and Embellishments on page 72 for helpful information before you start this or any project.

Black: Cut 1 rectangle 50" x 26" for the background (this is slightly oversized and will be cut to the finished size before binding).

Fabric for appliqué: Cut as needed.

Backing: Cut 1 rectangle 52" x 28".

Binding: Cut and piece 4 strips 2¼" wide to equal 160".

Tips for Making Giving Joy

1. Have the patterns on pages 34–35 enlarged 200% before you begin. See instructions for machine appliqué using fusible web on page 73. Trace all pattern pieces onto the fusible web following the instructions on page 73.

2. Cover your workspace to protect it before painting. Using the heavy gray lines on the pattern as guidelines, paint before you start fusing appliqué shapes to the background. Let the paint dry completely.

3. After fusing the web to the wrong side of the assorted bright fabric scraps, cut out the tree and gift shapes. Fuse and machine appliqué the shapes onto the background.

4. Glue braid to spell "JOY" and "GIVING" across the quilt top.

5. Embellish the shapes and words with decorative machine stitches and threads, fabric paints, gems, sequins, and beads.

6. Layer the quilt top with the batting and backing. Pin or thread-baste the layers together.

7. Quilt around each shape, then quilt geometric shapes and lines in the background.

8. Trim to the finished size and bind.

Enlarge 200%.

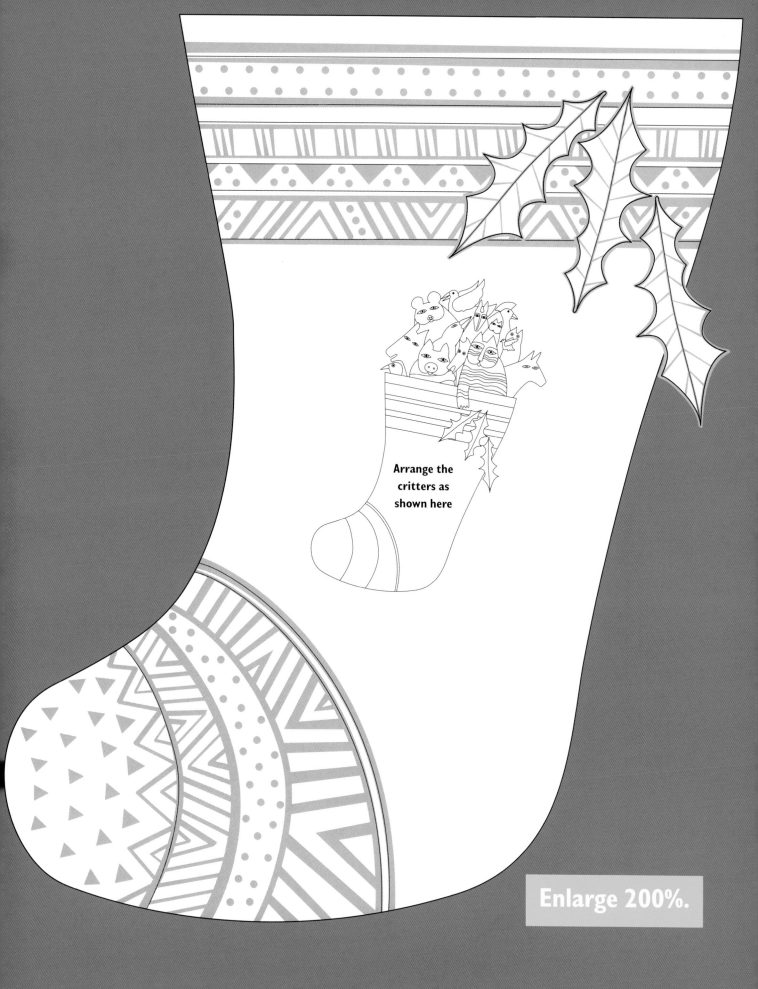

Arrange the
critters as
shown here

Enlarge 200%.

Magical
Winged Bunny

Finished Pillow Size: 12" x 18½"

Made by Charlene Dakin, Lafayette, CA, 2003. Felt graciously donated by National Nonwovens.

Materials

- Red felt: ⅜ yard for the pillow front
- White felt: ¼ yard for the wings
- Purple felt: ¼ yard for the bunny body
- Yellow felt: ⅛ yard for the bunny face
- Fuchsia felt: Very small scrap for the bunny tail

- Black felt: ⅜ yard for pillow back
- Fabric paints: Red, purple, white, and metallic blue and gold
- Black fabric pen, fine-point
- Threads for decorative stitching: Gold, black, and red

- Invisible thread
- Teal cording: 1¾ yards ⅛" wide
- Pillow form: 11" x 17"
- Pinking shears or pinking blade
- Fabric glue

Cutting

See Tips & Techniques for Appliqué and Embellishments on page 72 for helpful information before you start this or any project.

Red Felt: Cut 1 rectangle 13" x 19½". This measurement is slightly oversized. Trim to the finished size after the appliqué is complete.

Black Felt: Cut 1 rectangle 12" x 18".

Fabric for Appliqué: Cut as needed.

Tips for Making the Magical Winged Bunny Pillow

1. Have the pattern on page 42 enlarged 200% before you begin. See instructions for machine appliqué using fusible web on pages 72-73. Trace all pattern pieces onto the fusible web.

2. Cover your workspace to protect it before painting. Using the heavy gray lines on the pattern as guidelines. paint before you start fusing appliqué shapes to the background. Let the paint dry completely.

3. Arrange and pin the shapes to the red background. Machine appliqué each shape to the background and add embellishments.

4. Use the pinking shears or a pinking blade to trim the red background to 12" x 18½".

5. Use fabric glue to attach cording ½" away from the edge of the red background.

6. Center the red pillow front over the black pillow backing with wrong sides together.

Pin in place. Use invisible thread to zigzag over the cording and attach the pillow front to the back. Leave an opening to insert a pillow form.

7. Insert the pillow form into the opening. Pin and finish sewing to close the pillow cover.

Enlarge 200%.

joy • joy • joy • joy • joy

Enlarge 150%.

Dancing Dogs
Mantel Runner

Finished Size: 21" x 47½"

Machine appliquéd and quilted by Barbara Baker and Jeri Boe, Bend, OR, 2003.
Fabrics generously donated by FASCO/Clothworks.

Materials

- Bright scraps: for faces
- Pale gold: 1½ yards for background
- Multicolored print: ½ yard for dogs and stars
- White cotton lamé: ⅛
- yard for wings
- Backing: 1½ yards
- Binding: ¼ yard striped fabric
- Batting: 25" x 52"
- Fusible web: ½ yard
- Invisible thread
- Black fabric pen, fine-point
- Gold metallic fabric pen
- Fabric paint: White

Cutting

See Tips & Techniques for Appliqué and Embellishments on page 72 for helpful information before you start this or any project.

Pale Gold: Cut 1 rectangle 25" x 52".

Multicolored Print: Cut 2 dog 1 bodies.
Cut 2 dog 2 bodies.
Cut 4 dog heads with ears.

Cut 36 stars.

White Lamé: Cut 2 pairs of wings and 2 single wings.

Backing: Cut 1 rectangle 25" x 52".

Stripe: Cut and piece 4 strips 1¾" wide to equal 155" for the binding.

Tips for Making the Dancing Dogs Mantel Runner

1. Have the patterns on page 50 enlarged 200% before you begin. See instructions for machine appliqué using fusible web on page 72. Trace all pattern pieces onto the fusible web following the instructions on page 73.

2. Cover your workspace to protect it before painting. Using the heavy gray lines on the pattern as guidelines paint before you start fusing appliqué shapes to the background. Let the paint dry completely.

3. Fuse the shapes onto the background.

4. Use fabric pens to draw details.

5. Use invisible thread to machine appliqué the shapes to the background.

6. Layer the mantel runner, batting and backing. Pin or thread-baste the layers together.

7. Quilt the mantel runner in an all-over design.

8. Trim the mantel runner to 21" x 47½". Scallop the lower edge to echo the dogs' shapes.

9. Bind the mantel runner.

Dancing Dogs

dog 1

dog 2

Enlarge 200%.

Joyful Cats Tree Skirt

Finished Size: 39" diameter

Machine appliquéd and quilted by Barbara Baker and Jeri Boe, Bend, OR, 2003.
Fabrics generously donated by FASCO/Clothworks.

Materials

- Pale gold: 1⅛ yards for background
- Multicolored print: ½ yard for cats and stars
- Teal: ½ yard for cats
- Bright scraps: for faces
- White cotton lamé: ⅛ yard for wings
- Backing: 1¼ yards
- Binding: ⅓ yard striped fabric
- Batting: 43" diameter
- Fusible web: 1 yard
- Invisible thread
- Black fabric pen, fine-point
- Gold metallic fabric pen
- Fabric paint: White

Cutting

See Tips & Techniques for Appliqué and Embellishments on page 72 for helpful information before you start this or any project.

Pale Gold: Cut 1 circle 40" in diameter (radius 20").

Teal: Cut 3 cat 1 bodies.

Multicolored Print: Cut 3 cat 2 bodies.
Cut 6 cat heads.
Cut 22 small stars.
Cut 3 large stars.

White Lamé: Cut 12 wings.

Backing: Cut 1 circle 42" in diameter (radius 21"), or a circle that will fit within the width of the fabric (must be slightly larger than the skirt top).

Striped: Cut and piece 5 strips 1¾" wide to equal 200" for the binding.

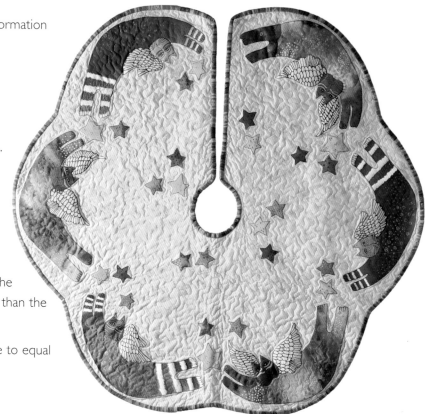

Tips for Making the Joyful Cats Tree Skirt

1. Have the Joyful Cats patterns on page 53 enlarged 200% before you begin. See instructions for using fusible web on page 73. Trace all pattern pieces onto the fusible web.

2. Cover your workspace to protect it before painting. Paint before you start fusing using the heavy gray appliqué shapes to the background. Let the paint dry completely.

3. Fuse the shapes onto the background.

4. Use fabric pens to draw details.

5. Use invisible thread to machine appliqué the shapes to the background.

6. Layer the tree skirt, batting, and backing. Pin or thread baste the layers together

7. Quilt the tree skirt in an all-over design.

8. Trim the tree skirt to a 39"-diameter circle (radius 19½"). Scallop the edge to echo the cats' shapes. Cut a slit between 2 cats to the center of the tree skirt. Cut a 4¾"-diameter circle (radius 2⅜") in the center of the tree skirt.

9. Bind the scalloped edge and central slit of the tree skirt.

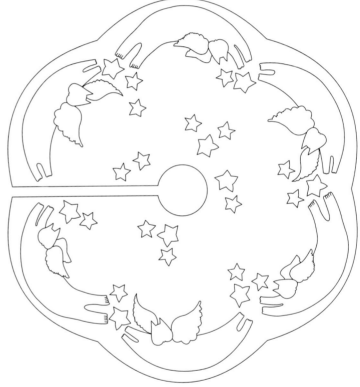

Joyful Cats

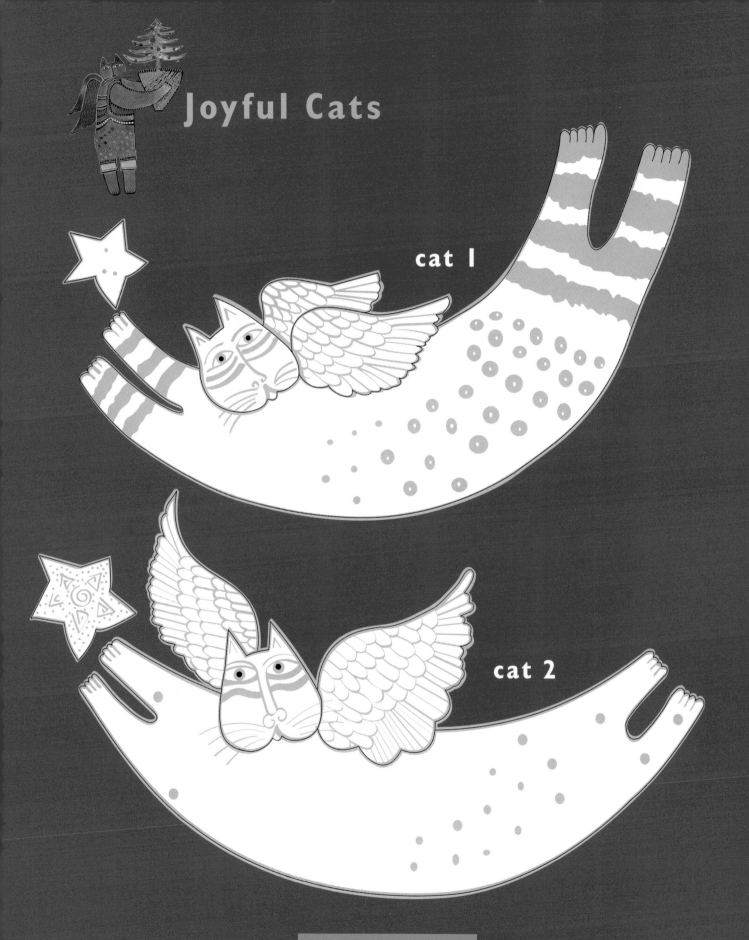

cat 1

cat 2

Enlarge 200%.

Very Special
Ornament Collection

All ornaments made by Christine Batterman, San Ramon, California, 2003.

Materials for Painted Glass Ornaments

- Clear round glass ornament
- Carbon paper or dressmaker's chalk paper
- Glossy acrylic craft paint
- Trims: Ribbons, bells, and flowers
- Hot glue gun

Tips for Making the Painted Glass Christmas Tree Ornaments

1. Cover your workspace to protect it before painting. Let the paint dry completely before attaching the trims.

2. Paint the ornament with the background color and let dry.

3. Place carbon paper or dressmaker's chalk paper on the painted ornament. Place the pattern over the carbon or chalk paper. Trace over the lines of the pattern with a ballpoint pen or round-point stiletto.

4. Paint the pattern design following the carbon or chalk outline.

5. Use a hot glue gun to attach the trims.

Note: The patterns on page 55 can be used to make glass, felt, or machine-appliquéd cotton ornaments.

Starlight Forest
Table Runner

Finished Table Runner Size: 15" x 56"

Machine appliquéd and quilted by Christine Batterman, San Ramon, CA, 2003. Fabrics generously donated by Blank Textiles.

Materials for Table Runner

- Black tone-on-tone: ⅜ yard for center block back ground
- Blue polka dot: ⅛ yard for trees
- Yellow polka dot: ⅛ yard for trees
- Green polka dot: ⅛ yard for trees
- A variety of prints to total ¼ yard for tree trunks pieced sashing, and borders
- Rainbow variegated: ¼ yard for inner borders
- Black print: ½ yard for outer borders
- Backing: 1 ⅝ yard
- Binding: ¼ yard
- Batting: 19" x 60"
- Fusible web: 1 yard
- Variegated thread

Cutting

See Tips & Techniques for Appliqué and Embellishments on page 72 for helpful information before you start this or any project.

Black Tone-on-tone: Cut 4 rectangles 9" x 11½" for center block backgrounds.

Blue Polka Dot: Cut 12 triangles.

Yellow Polka Dot: Cut 16 triangles.

Green Polka Dot: Cut 12 triangles.

Variety of Print Scraps: Cut 12 tree trunks. Cut 60 squares 1½" x 1½".

Rainbow Variegated: Cut 8 strips 1" x 11½" for top and bottom inner borders.
Cut 8 strips 1" x 10" for side inner borders.

Black print: Cut 8 strips 1¾" x 12½" for sashing between blocks.
Cut 2 strips 1¾" x 15" for top and bottom sashing.
Cut 2 strips 1¾" x 53½" for side outer borders.

Binding: Cut and piece 4 strips 1¾" wide to total 155".

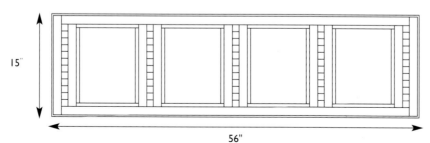

Tips for Making the Starlight Forest Table Runner

1. Have the pattern on page 62 enlarged 250% before you begin. See instructions for machine appliqué using fusible web on page 73. Trace all pattern pieces onto the fusible web following the instructions.

2. Fuse the tree shapes to the block backgrounds.

3. Use variegated thread to machine appliqué the tree shapes to the backgrounds.

4. Sew the top and bottom inner borders to the blocks. Press the seams toward the borders.

5. Sew the side inner borders to the blocks. Press the seams toward the borders.

6. Sew together end-to-end 12 scrappy squares to make a pieced sashing strip. Press. Make 4 more pieced sashing strips.

7. Sew a black print sashing strip to each side of 3 pieced sashing strips. Sew a black print sashing strip to 1 side of the other 2 pieced sashing strips. Press seams toward black print sashing strips.

8. Alternately sew the 5 black and pieced sashing strips to the 4 tree blocks. Press.

9. Sew the side outer borders to the table runner and press the seams toward the outer borders.

10. Sew the top and bottom sashing borders to the table runner. Press the seams toward the sashing.

11. Layer the table runner, batting and backing. Pin or thread-baste the layers together.

12. Quilt in-the-ditch around the trees and along the black outer border.

13. Trim, square, and bind the table runner.

Photo by Garry Gay

Starlight Forest
Placemats

Finished Placemat Size: 12½" x 17¼"

Materials for 4 Placemats

- Black tone-on-tone: ⅜ yard for background
- Blue polka dot: ⅛ yard
- Yellow polka dot: ⅛ yard
- Green polka dot: ⅛ yard
- A variety of prints to total ¼ yard for tree trunks
- and pieced side outer borders
- Rainbow variegated: ¼ yard for inner border
- Black print: ½ yard for middle border
- Backing: ⅞ yard
- Binding: ½ yard blue print
- Batting: 14" x 20" for each placemat
- Fusible web: 1 yard
- Variegated thread

Cutting

See Tips & Techniques for Appliqué and Embellishments on page 72 for helpful information before you start this or any project.

Note: The following is for 1 placemat.

Black Tone-on-tone: Cut 1 rectangle 9" x 11¾" for background.

Blue Polka Dot: Cut 3 triangles.

Yellow Polka Dot: Cut 4 triangles.

Green Polka Dot: Cut 3 triangles.

Variety of Print Scraps: Cut 3 tree trunks. Cut 24 squares 1½" x 1½".

Rainbow Variegated:
Cut 2 strips 1" x 11¾" for top and bottom inner borders.
Cut 2 strips 1" x 10" for side inner borders.

Black Print: Cut 2 strips 1¾" x 12¾" for top and bottom outer borders.
Cut 2 strips 1¾" x 12½" for side middle borders.

Backing: Cut 1 rectangle 14" x 20".

Binding: Cut and piece 2 strips 1¾" wide to total 71".

Tips for Making the Starlight Forest Placemats

1. Have the pattern on page 62 enlarged 250% before you begin. See instructions for machine appliqué using fusible web on page 73. Trace all pattern pieces onto the fusible web.

2. Fuse the tree shapes to the background.

3. Use variegated thread to machine appliqué the shapes to the background.

4. Sew the top and bottom rainbow inner borders to the placemat and press the seams toward the borders.

5. Sew the side rainbow inner borders to the placemat and press the seams toward the borders.

6. Sew the top and bottom black print outer borders to the placemat and press the seams toward the outer borders.

7. Sew the side black print middle borders to the placemat and press the seams toward the middle borders.

8. Sew together end-to-end 12 scrappy squares to make a pieced sashing strip. Press the seams in one direction. Make 1 more pieced sashing strip.

9. Sew the pieced sashing strips to the black print middle borders. Press the seams toward the middle borders.

10. Layer the placemat, batting, and backing. Pin or thread-baste the layers together.

11. Quilt in-the-ditch around the trees and along the border seams.

12. Trim, square, and bind the placemat. Repeat the above steps to make the remaining 3 placemats.

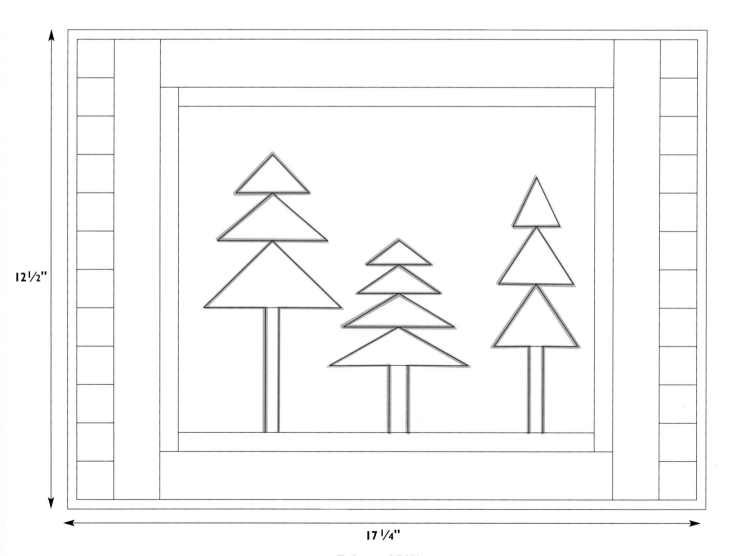

12½"

17¼"

Enlarge 250%.

Starlight Forest Vest

Just add a few trees from *Giving Joy* to jazz up a purchased vest.

Materials

- Purchased vest
- Scraps of bright print or solid fabrics
- Fusible web
- Variegated thread
- Gold fabric paint

Tips for Making the Vest

1. Trace the pattern pieces onto fusible web. Fuse onto scraps chosen for trees.

2. Fuse the tree shapes to the vest.

3. Use variegated thread to machine appliqué the shapes to the background.

4. Add details and outlines with fabric paint.

Dear Santa Embroidered Shirt

What a great and easy gift: Embroider a purchased shirt with a Laurel Burch holiday design such as this colorful Santa Paws.

Materials

- Purchased turtleneck shirt or other blouse
- Studio Bernina Fantastic Felines Embroidery package
- 40-weight polyester embroidery thread
- Sewing machine with embroidery module

Tips for Making the Dear Santa Shirt

1. Review the thread colors recommended for the design you will stitch out, such as Dear Santa. Thread colors may be changed as desired.

2. Lightly mark the area of the shirt to embroider.

3. Follow your manual to set up your hoop, stabilizer, and shirt, and then to stitch the design. Enjoy!

Dear Santa Tote Bag

Finished Size of Pocket: 10" x 12 ½"

Machine appliquéd, quilted, and embellished by Lyda McAuliff, Pleasanton, California, 2003.

Fabric generously donated by Marcus Brothers.

Materials

- Unfinished or purchased tote bag (Measure area for pocket first; add or resize borders if needed to fit area.)
- Black: ⅓ yard for background
- Gold cotton lamé: Scraps

- Batik and bright fabrics: scraps of magenta, blue, purple, red, white, green, orange, brown, and black
- Batting: 11" x 13½"
- Backing: ⅜ yard
- Fusible web: ¼ yard
- Thread for decorative stitching: Gold and black

- Gold braid, ⅛" wide: 1½ yards
- Fabric paint for eyes: Brown
- Fabric puff paint: Gold and red
- Black fabric pen

Cutting

See Tips & Techniques for Appliqué and Embellishments on page 72 for helpful information before you start this or any project.

Black: Cut 1 rectangle 8" x 11" for background.

Gold Cotton Lamé: Cut 2 strips 1⅛" x 12⅛" for outer side borders.
Cut 1 strip, ⅞" x 10½" for outer top border.
Cut 1 strip 1" x 10½" for outer bottom border.

Blue: Cut 2 strips 1⅛" x 11" for the inner side borders.

Magenta: Cut 1 strip 1⅛" x 9¼" for the inner top border.

Green: Cut 1 strip 1" x 9¼" for the inner bottom border.

Fabrics for Appliqué: Cut as needed.

Backing: Cut 1 rectangle 11" x 13½".

Tips for Making the Dear Santa Tote Bag

1. The pattern on page 67 is full size and ready for use to make the pocket on the front of the bag. See instructions for machine appliqué using fusible web on page 73.

2. Cover your workspace to protect it before painting. Paint before you start fusing appliqué shapes to the background. Let the paint dry completely.

3. Fuse the shapes to the background. Use decorative threads to machine stitch the shapes to the black background. Embellish the design with additional decorative stitching, fabric paints, and fabric pens.

4. Sew gold braid to the background to spell "Dear Santa."

5. Assemble the pocket as shown in the photo on page 64, pressing the seams toward the borders.

If the pocket is being attached to an unfinished tote bag, use the following directions:

1. Trim the appliquéd pocket to square the corners.

2. Place the backing right side down on the right side of the pocket. Place the batting on top of the backing. Trim the batting and backing to match the pocket front.

3. Sew across the top and bottom of the pocket, through the batting and backing. Trim the seams and turn the batting and backing to the back of the pocket. Press.

4. Baste the batting and backing to the pocket front along the sides.

5. Use decorative thread to machine quilt in-the-ditch between the background of the design and the inner borders. Quilt a parallel line in the top outer border.

6. Pin the pocket to the front of the tote bag. Use decorative thread to sew 2 parallel lines in the lower outer border of the pocket and attach it to the tote bag.

7. Sew the tote bag straps over the sides of the pocket to cover the unfinished edges.

If the pocket is being attached to a premade tote bag, use the following directions:

1. Trim the pocket to square the corners.

2. Place the backing right side down on the right side of the pocket. Place the batting on top of the backing. Trim the batting and backing to match the pocket front.

3. Sew ¼" away from the edge on all 4 sides, leaving a small opening at the bottom for turning. Trim the seam. Turn the pocket right side out. Sew the opening closed.

4. Use decorative thread to machine quilt in-the-ditch between the background of the design and the inner borders. Quilt 1 parallel line in the top and 2 lines in the bottom outer borders.

5. Sew the pocket to the tote bag.

Wings of a Dove Felt Wreath

Finished Size: 27" x 14" (approximate)

Made by Lynn Koolish, Berkeley, California, 2003. Felt generously donated by National Nonwovens.

Materials

- Dark green felt: 1 yard for the arch base or purchase an evergreen swag
- Light green felt: ¼ yard for holly leaves
- Fuchsia felt: ¼ yard

- Orange felt: 6" x 6" square
- Red-orange felt: 5" x 8" rectangle
- Red buttons, ½" diameter: 12
- Polyfil
- Fusible web: 1 yard

- Thread for decorative stitching: Gold and green
- Fabric paint: Red, yellow, blue, purple, gold, and black
- Fabric glue or hot glue gun
- Decorative cord: ½ yard

Cutting

Dark Green Felt: Cut 2 arch bases and 8 half-holly leaves.

Light Green Felt: Cut 34 holly leaves and 8 half-holly leaves.

Fuchsia Felt: Cut 2 bird shapes and larger wings.

Orange Felt: Cut beak and middle wing.

Red-orange Felt: Cut upper wings.

Tips for Making the Wings of a Dove Felt Wreath

1. The patterns on page 70 are full size and ready for use to trace the dove and the holly leaves. Use the shape and the overall dimensions of the arch shape to create a full size background arch. See instructions for machine appliqué using fusible web on pages 72-73. Trace all pattern pieces onto the fusible web.

2. Cover your workspace to protect it before painting. Paint before you start fusing appliqué shapes to the background. Let the paint dry completely.

3. Pin the 2 arch bases wrong sides together and topstitch ⅛" away from the edges with the green thread. Leave an opening for stuffing.

4. Firmly stuff the arch base with the Polyfil. Finish sewing the arch base.

5. Fuse 26 light green holly leaves together to make 13 holly leaves.

6. To make the two-tone holly leaves fuse a light green half-holly leaf and a dark green half-holly leaf onto a full holly leaf as a base Make 8 two-tone leaves.

7. Sew ⅛" inside the edge of each leaf using metallic thread, and sew veins in the center of each leaf.

8. Handstitch each leaf onto the arch base.

9. Fuse the 2 bird shapes wrong sides together. Embellish 1 side with fabric paint.

10. Sew ⅛" inside the edges. Sew parallel lines on the tail feathers.

11. Use fabric glue to assemble the bird.

12. Handstitch the bird to the arch.

13. Stitch clusters of buttons onto the arch to resemble holly berries.

14. Center and stitch the decorative cord in a loop on the back of the arch.

Wings of a Dove

Arch

27"

14"

Leaf Pattern

Dove Pattern